AFTERGLOW

Also by Martin C. Rosner

AFTERGLOW

Poems by Martin C. Rosner, M. D.

New Alexandria Press
Livonia

Published by New Alexandria Press
PO Box 530516
Livonia, Michigan 48153
www.newalexandriapress.com

Softcover Edition:
ISBN-10: 1-60916-0023-5
ISBN-13: 978-1-60915-023-5

Quantity discounts are available on bulk purchases of this book
Special books or book excerpts can also be made available to fit
specific needs. For information, please contact
sales@newalexandriapress.com or send written inquiries to New
Alexandria Press, PO Box 530516, Livonia, Michigan 48153.

Printed in the United States of America

10 9 8 7 6 5 4 3 2 1

For my wife Arlene,
  who has always been the poetry in my life....

Table of Contents

Afterglow. 3
Retrospective. 4
On My Birthday. 6
Age and Time. 7
Enigma. 8
Nostalgia. 9
At Dusk. 10
Entropy. 11
Dead Reckoning. 12
Mirage. 13
The Cosmic Lock. 14
The Redoubt. 16
Ebb Tide. 17
Weather Forecast. 18
The Bronx, World War 2. 20
Unanswerable. 23
The Silkie. 24
1958. 25
The Question. 26
Kaddish. 27
The Portrait. 28
Between The Worlds. 30
The Message In The Wind. 31
Transformation. 32
The Voyage. 33

Foreword

If, as others have observed, poetry is music set to words, then poets enjoy a special place in the world of creative arts. Blending human language into images and sounds that evoke living sparks of imagination in the minds of their audience, poetry has followed humans from the campfires of our primitive ancestors to the glittering streets of our modern world. And yet there is something mysterious, almost magical, about the way the cadences and rhythms of the spoken word can speak to the human soul, letting voices long passed echo in the hearts of those still living.

But however deep or profound it may be, thoughts and sentiments die with us unless they are shared with others. Like other writers, poets share a unique bond with their readers, in that their voices can live far beyond the lifetimes of the speaker. But in the imagination of a gifted poet, words can transcend the limits that language places on most of us, as the image-rich music that lies dormant in our spoken words comes to life in the sparkle and dance of new-born images and off-beat insights of an artist at play, confronting the human condition through its absurdities and tragedies.

In *Afterglow*, the latest collection of the poetry of Martin Rosner, we see the rich insights of a mature poet, viewing life through a prism of approaching mortality. As always, the insights are vivid and fresh. And, as always, they are unfettered by illusion. It's been a pleasure working on the collection; I hope that the reader enjoys reading them as much as I've enjoyed helping to put them together.

Jeffrey Caminsky

AFTERGLOW

Afterglow

At night when pain descends
And sadness wraps me
In its cloak, I journey
To another time and place
To meet my other self.
He does not know that he is I
But I know that I am he.
I cannot change his future,
He cannot change my past.
So it's kinder not to press him hard,
To let him find his way.
Eventually he will join me
To take my place today.

Retrospective

Increasingly, I am a spectator.
I see the world as slides
Viewed through a stereopticon,
People fixed in place, silent,
Closing out their empty words,
The rage, the pain, confusion
Surging through the tortured air,
Broadcast like a storm
Of sound, stifling the music
Of the wind, the birds,
The language of the waves.
You say I am retreating,
That I am wrapping up
My feelings to avoid
The clamor of humanity,
The ceaseless din
Of history unfolding
Like the swelling chorus
Of a dirge.
You say that I walk backwards
Towards the future,
Unable to shield my eyes
From the horrors of the past,

Knowing that they penetrate
The illusion of the present,
That those who walk
Beside me are anesthetized
Just enough to dull
The searing truth
Which would consume them
Like a sudden blast of flame.
But I am no coward,
Just old enough to know
That you are right.

On My Birthday

I am an ant
Trying to move a mountain
Tugging at a wrinkle in time
To prove that courage
Is its own reward .
The earth has journeyed
'Round the sun two
And eighty times
Since I first awakened
To my growing ignorance,
And all I've learned
Is that the other ants
Are mostly ignorant
Of their dismal ignorance.
So if the universe
Took passing notice
Of the speck
On which we strive
Perhaps it would conclude
Both us and our hubris
To bring order to its work.

Age and Time

Chinese, Japanese and Native Americans
Gave honor to the aged
For their achievements
And accumulated wisdom.
Old poets Yeats and Masefield
Wrote the words that mourn
Our modern brash neglect
Of those we should admire
As the builders of our lives.
We commemorate their passing
With mingled sadness and relief
Like pall bearers setting down
A very heavy load.
The leaning headstones in the weeds
And the lonely ash-filled urns
Are more and more forgotten
In the flood of mundane life,
Except for wiser spirits
Who know that they are next.

Enigma

I have mislaid my touchstones.
They always glowed to show
The clearly destined path I had to walk.
Now I stumble weakly
On a dark uncertain road
That leads along a ravaged
Landscape towards an end
I neither want nor understand.
Who gave them to me
And why they disappeared
Are mysteries I cannot know.
I hope their magic transferred
Through the sorcery
That briefly guides us
In the labyrinth of life
To an eager hand that grasps
Them and kindles them to life
As mine did
When I was young.

Nostalgia

There are words that conjure up nostalgia,
Like opening an old beloved book.
Feelings rising with the sweetness
And the sense of loss that lingers
As a gentle floral scent that passes
With the poignance of a sudden
Summer breeze that briefly lingers
On a dune above the sea.
Sad words, intermingled beauty and regret,
A burst of feelings bright
And dark, complex as a mosaic
On an ancient temple wall.
Like that wall, the feelings
Fade into the past, encompassing
All that signifies by saying,
"When I was young".

At Dusk

Call me greedy, for my lease on life
Is long, well past the day
When I could walk with grace,
And hard men looked away, and ladies
Smiled when I strode along the street.
Now I am reduced to recollections,
And they are just a jest,
A ruse the gods can use
To lift their boredom in eternity.
So knowing this, why do I persist?
Because a meteor flames a microsecond
In the frozen blackness of the void,
But its light is never lost.

Entropy

So now I've come to a place
I never thought I'd see,
A place that I never imagined
Nor believed that I would be.
It's where clear certainty
Dissolves into obscurity,
Where wisdom falters and withdraws
And sheer absence of control
Looms like phantoms growing whole.
Shall I struggle, thrash and fight
Or trust my intuition
To show my true position
And guide me towards the light?

Dead Reckoning

Sitting on a friendly log,
Half way through my morning
Walk, I gaze along the road
On which I came, but instead
Perceive the vastly greater
Distance of the past.
So I realize, my feet which
Seemingly touch the ground,
Are really hanging over
An abyss I cannot bring
To focus or even comprehend.
Much like a murky night
At sea, when lightening strikes
Illuminate the rolling, trackless
Waves, the years have taught me
To look bravely at the flashes,
To cherish the light
That accompanies the fright,
And leaves me still on course.

Mirage

I still live between marsh and sea,
But the rest of the world
Shimmers and changes daily,
Hanging at the tip
Of the wizard's wand.
Where there were people
There are shape-changers,
Girls morphed into crones,
Men into bent or bloated
Cartoons for a Hallowe'en fright.
I go to my mirror, to admonish
The monster who lives there.
I command him to disappear,
In a voice of imperial command
Somehow fuzzed with phlegm.
He smiles and tells me
All that would leave
Is an empty glass.

The Cosmic Lock

Wisdom is elusive and evades
The glib purveyors in the marketplace.
Even scholars, religious visionaries
And scientists wander trails
That trap them in the labyrinth
Of mirrors, illusions and deceptions
That snakes from Newton,
Einstein and the quantum world
To culminate where it began.
So is the universe and life
And man himself unfathomable,
Or shall we comfort ourselves
With poisoned apples
That our savants claim
To be the fruits of total
Understanding, which we never
Should deny, that will lase
The cosmic lock?
But we make the same mistakes
That snake throughout our history
And constitute the hubris of our pride.

Round and round the mulberry bush
The primate chased his shadow
Stepping on it all the way.
Pop goes the shadow.

The Redoubt

I am not yet broken.
My limbs are stiff,
My organs mock my will.
The quicksilver warrior
I used to be, lives on
In the minds of aged men
Whose need to recollect
Sustains their darkening days
And mine.
But I am not yet broken,
Nor will I be
So long as I can rouse
The smouldering flame
That flickers in my inner sense of self.
I feed the shrinking fire
So that I will call
One final act of strength
When the final battle breaks
And looms to to overwhelm
My last defiant stand
But proves that faith and courage
Were not in vain.

Ebb Tide

Apart from the tumultuous world,
This sacred place of sea and sky
And marsh, has calmed the clamor
Of my youth, the chaos
In my middle years, and now
It stills the hiss of ebb tide
In my spirit's slowing stream.
Somehow in this scene the intolerable
Inevitable is almost acceptable.
But deep within my heart
A rebel pulse still beats,
And I am angry,
And I will not yield.

Weather Forecast

Treetops polish the pewter sky
Which promises rain, or foretells
Vengeance day.
That which orders the weather
Of the world
May be indifferent to the quantity
Of each
But scorns our concentration
On the former
And our willful welcome
To the other choice.
Perhaps in distant galaxies
Another species
Much like us, but wiser,
Polishes a sky like ours
But evolved to understand
That rain is part of life
But vengeance cannot be.
If so, where did we so fatally
Turn wrong
Climbing up the evolutionary tree?

That tragic turning must have been
To creep along the branch
That left us hanging free
But could not bear our weight.

The Bronx, World War 2

When I was young I lived
Inside a man-made mountain
In a cave with heat, indoor
Plumbing and windows
Through which I watched
The wild life in the streets.
My tribe lived in the mountain,
Or in nearby mountains
To which I walked, always
Wary of the predators
Who moved singly or in groups,
Sometimes with knives,
Much like the feral dogs
Who nosed the garbage
In the alleys or on the curbs.
But I was not afraid,
Because I gloried in my running
Speed, and besides, I was
A famous warrior, who
They seldom would confront.
I knew that I was poor,

But my mother foraged daily
In the dingy markets
Where the chickens waited
To be killed, and fish
Swam in tanks, netted
To be sacrificed for holidays,
Brilliant with the rare
Delights, like little chocolate turkeys,
Candy apples and whipped cream cakes.
At Christmas lights adorned the grimy windows
And bells and carols sanctified the streets.
El Dorado was the public library,
Housing treasures inconceivable
To conquistadores and adventurers,
But the storied wealth
Invisible to those
Who did not mine that hoard.
I knew that I was poor,
That I could only peer
With wistfulness through shop fronts.
But my clothing, warm but shabby

Was adorned with stick pin buttons
Showing generals and leaders
Of the country I so loved.
And the classrooms were
My magic ladder, to climb
To be a scholar, soldier,
Doctor and a poet
Who speaks to you
In melancholy tones,
Because I know that
I was richer than my children
Or their offspring
Who live in luxury
Unimaginable to futurists
And seers of that time.
That is so, because the precious
Hallowed values that grew
And flourished then
Are fading, along with me,
Into the past.

Unanswerable

My world no longer has a rounded shape.
The giant cutting blade of fate
Facets it constantly.
Now it is a polyhedral New Year's globe,
Slowly sinking towards the ground,
Reflecting last year's light
For celebrants already gone.
Faint echoes of the party music
Linger, as it makes its way
Through space, to mingle
With the voices and the singing
That have gone before.
My question then, is whether
These vibrations, and the flakes
Chipped off my world, are conserved
In some mysterious process
That activates the universe,
Or do they journey on eternally
Towards transformation inconceivable,
Indestructible.

The Silkie

I used to be amphibian,
A creature from the sea,
A man upon the land,
A seal upon the sea.
Humans called me silkie,
A seal in human form.
They sang I walked among them
Searching for a bride.
And maidens walked the ocean's edge,
Peering through the grey sea mist,
Hoping it would coalesce
In answer to their plea.
But years have dried men's memories,
Only Celts remember me.
In Scotland and in Ireland
The old tell tales of me.
Their faith sustains my breath
To linger by their sea.
But as the few grow fewer
My seal soul shrinks in me.
When the last believer dies
The sea will close to me.

1958

Sometimes the image in the mirror
Blurs, and morphs into a younger
Man, wearing a blue uniform
With silver railroad tracks
Upon each sturdy shoulder.
Who was that man, thunderbolt,
Lightening rod, proud defender
Of the great republic, unique
In deed and concept,
Overarching the grateful world?
He was an antique sculpture,
Like the Greek and Roman
Relics in museums, unrelated
To a nation and a world
That snickers at the epics
And rewrites the stories
Of a disappearing time
So that nobility is subtracted
Except on those official days
Of hypocritical observance
Which everyone can easily
Endure, and then return
To listening to their I-Pods
And reading solemn disavowals
Of the history he made.

The Question

Long ago I loved a book
about a reddleman who
walked across a giant heath
to sell his dye at isolated
cottages that pocked the land.
He had no company but earth
and sky, and the soaring birds,
although from time to time
a shy young girl would welcome him
at the threshold of her tiny house.
While alone, he was not lonely,
but reveled in his peace and freedom
which he knew was dearly bought
but never thought the price too high.
Now when I think about his choice
it makes me question,
just as then, how to find the balance
between a life like that
and the turmoil that we live today.
But the answer still eludes me,
waiting still across the endless heath.

Kaddish

Lamentations, lamentations fill
The temple of my mind,
Plangent with grief.
Not for me, not for me,
Nor even for my friends
Who limp their painful way
Along the steep descending road,
But for the voices in the winds
Of history, all the nameless
Sufferers who came before,
Now stifled in obscurity,
Their torment unrecalled.
I never knew them, although
I feel they were my kin.
Now their reproaches, bleeding
Through the centuries,
Assail me to exhort
For recollection, justice, sorrow
And compassion, while the deafened
Ears, the small dry selfish minds
Refuse to hear their cries.
Thus I must mourn
For they will not.

The Portrait

Rarely, like waking from a disappearing dream,
Drifting drowsily down museum corridors,
A woman's face within a portrait looks
Directly out with meaning, searching
From another century and place,
And in her link with me
Collapses time and space.
Hundreds of years are the previous
Moment, and she seems about to speak
In lyric language, drawn
From her brimming heart,
Words of mystical truth.
But before she does, the air
Is filled with static, coming
From her guardians, my jailers,
Custodians of the cosmic laws
That lock us in the prison
Of the present.
We batter at its walls
Like a moth against a windowpane
Beguiled by visions dimly seen

Through misty glass.
We glimpse the evanescent,
Exquisite connection, reaching
From another present, but fading
Into canvas, paint, and frame.
Someone else's long forgotten dream.

Between The Worlds

So long I have lived in this body,
So long I have lived in this world,
But I only have rented them both,
And my lease keeps changing, inexplicably.
I do not need a lawyer or a linguist
To understand, nor even a physicist,
Mathematician, physician or philosopher,
But a sorcerer who comprehends
The underlying magic, cosmic and quantum,
That animates it all.
Only he can lift the spell
That leaves my lonely consciousness
Isolated, without certain home
Or place.

The Message In The Wind

Lingering on my lonely log,
Embraced by sky, sea and marsh,
I hear no sound except the wind
Which mocks me wordlessly.
It speaks no language
But nonetheless is unmistakable
Although it comes from nowhere,
As have I, and goes somewhere
I cannot comprehend, but doubtless
I will follow there, as it insists.
It calls me superannuated member
Of an evanescent species
That thinks it is the capstone
Of creation, but is just
A closing pinprick in the cosmic
Tapestry that stretches on forever.
Listen, says the wind, and you will know
That mysterious, inconceivable design
Is the work of huge and restless forces
Which are never still.

Transformation

I am old, but the marsh
Is so much older,
Yet we have bonded through
The years that I have aged,
And it remains serenely changeless,
Retaining the cosmic elixir
That endows it as a womb.
The spicy, musky odor it emits
Is that of life transforming
From decay encoded inexplicably
By some supremely mystic force.
I hope it operates for man
As well as the other creatures
Generated in the marsh and on this earth
That we vainly strive to understand.
At last I must accept
That like the marsh,
Earth demands decay
In order to create new life.

The Voyage

I am overboard in open sea,
My empty little boat, serenely
Sailing out of sight, towards
Prospects I will never see.
Somehow I seem to understand
That all the years I thought
I was on land were really
On the sea, in an empty
Little boat, that was only
Lent to me.
It was mine for a time,
Though how that came to be
I do not know, and where
It's going I will never be.
So now I float and wait
And look from sky to sea,
Waiting to awaken from the dream
Or sink back to sleep
To the depths that I call me

About the Author

Martin C. Rosner is a board-certified specialist in Internal Medicine and Fellow of the American College of Cardiology, the American College of Angiology and the Royal Society of Health.

He has had five books of poetry published previously and poems in many newspapers, magazines, poetry journals and anthologies, including seventeen poems in *The New York Times*, and also *The Cape Codder, The Hartford Courant* and *The Stars and Stripes*. Dr. Rosner has won the prize for the best love lyric from Western Poetry Magazine. He is a member of the Academy of American Poets and is listed in Poets and Writers.

Dr. Rosner lives in Paramus, New Jesey with his wife of 60 years. He has three children and numerous grandchildren. The poet's favorite respite from medical practice for the past four decades years has been his house on Cape Cod Bay from where much of his poetry takes inspiration.